BALTIC HOMES
INSPIRATIONAL INTERIORS FROM NORTHERN EUROPE

Sølvi dos Santos
Laura Gutman-Hanhivaara

With 262 colour illustrations

Thames & Hudson

Norwegian Sea

FINLAND

Gulf of Bothnia

SWEDEN

NORWAY

Oslo ■

Uppsala ■

Ekskär
187 ★

Turku ■
207 ★
199 ★ Helsink

31 ★ 47
★
Stockholm

Haapsalu ■

173
★
Saaremaa

P ■

161 ★

Fårö
53 ★ 39 ★
★
63

Gotland

Kipsala
151 ★

★
Riga

Baltic Sea

DENMARK

Copenhagen ■
73
★
Ystad ★

Juodkrante 141
★ **LITHUANIA**
Curonian Spit

North Sea

83 ★

★ *Bornholm*
95

Vilni ■

123
Hiddensee ★ *Rügen*

Sopot
131
★

107
Travemünde ★

★
Lübeck ■ 113   **Germany**

Gdańsk ■

POLAND

Contents

Baltic Vistas

Some winters you could practically cross it on foot. When the Baltic Sea freezes over it becomes a vast white sheet, utterly silent, penetrated only by the massive bulk of ice-breakers.

PAGE 1: Sunrise over Haapsalu Bay, Estonia.
PAGES 2–3: Fishermen's huts on the west coast of Fårö, Sweden.
OPPOSITE: The museum at Fårösund on the island of Gotland, Sweden.

This unusual sweetness, due to the large rivers that drain their contents into the Baltic basin, means that the fishing is particularly good, with an abundance of sea and freshwater varieties alike. The coastal regions, like the islands and archipelagos, were inhabited until the 19th century by a scattering of fishermen and peasants. On the heathlands by the sea, sheep and horses have since time immemorial grazed the sparsely growing grass – a sharp contrast to the undulating plantations of rye, corn and flax that extend across the vast plain linking Germany, Poland and the Baltic lands. The farmhouses and fishermen's cottages were quite primitive constructions built of wood from the surrounding forests, and even the manor houses presiding over the various estates afforded no more than a modest degree of comfort. The towns of the Hanseatic League, built on river estuaries, sought to protect themselves against raids from the sea by erecting vast fortifications, above which the belltowers and gables of their town halls loomed up like landmarks for ships out at sea.

The history of the Baltic countries is that of a series of migrations and maritime conquests. The earliest explorers were the Vikings or Varangians who set out from present-day Sweden, Norway and Denmark, sometime before AD 800, and ventured as far as the coasts of Finland and Courland. Dealing in amber, skins and furs, they established a trading post at Visby on the island of Gotland. From the site of St Petersburg they travelled up the Neva to found the town and later principality of Novgorod, which was the origin of modern Russia (from Rus, or land of the 'red men' from Scandinavia).

In the 12th and 13th centuries, after they were converted to Christianity, the Danes pursued their colonial ambitions along the sea coast under the pretext of conducting a crusade against the pagans. By this means they captured Scania and the island of Rügen, established bases in Pomerania and later extended their possessions in Estonia. The magnificent 'age of the Valdemars' (1157–1241) saw the founding of both Copenhagen and Tallinn ('town of the Danes'). The founding of Lübeck in 1158–59 by Henry of Saxony provided a base for German merchants to expand their activities into the Baltic basin, where they established a series of outposts for their various companies. These were overseen by associates, often family members, who represented their interests in the new trading 'counters'. Riga and Königsberg (Kaliningrad), founded in 1201 and 1255 respectively, and Danzig (Gdańsk) and Reval (Tallinn), acquired in 1309 and 1346, were among the fortified towns under the control of German overlords who formed part of the Hanseatic League.

The last obstacle to the Christianization of the region was the pagan Grand Duchy of Lithuania, which extended as far as the Black Sea. In 1395, with the aim of denying the Teutonic Knights the pretext of mounting a crusade against them, the country adopted the Catholic religion and formed a union with the kingdom of Poland. With the decline of the League, in the 16th century the battle for control of the region was waged anew, this time between Denmark and Sweden, which had both become Protestant, Poland, which had remained Catholic, and Orthodox Russia. In the 17th century, under the Vasas, Sweden became the dominant force in the Baltic, which was almost transformed into a 'Swedish lake'.

In the 18th century, the Swedish spoils were divided between the German states and the Russia of Peter the Great, who founded St Petersburg and annexed the Baltic provinces. A century later, Napoleon and Tsar Alexander III joined forces to launch an attack on the last of the Swedish possessions, and Russia seized Finland. Under the Tsar's authority, Estonians, Livonians (Latvians), Lithuanians and Finns experienced broadly the same fate as the Russians themselves, while Poland, split between Germany, Austria and Russia, disappeared off the map altogether.

As a consequence of World War I and the Bolshevik Revolution, Russia was forced to withdraw from the region, and the 1920s saw the emergence of the new nations of Lithuania, Latvia, Estonia and Finland. The Nazi–Soviet Pact of 1939 brought this brief interval of freedom to a tragic end. Annexed by the USSR, they were occupied by Germany and came once again under Soviet domination. Their independence was restored in the so-called 'singing revolution' of 1991, which paved the way for entry to the European Union in 2004.

The Baltic lands are the common heirs to a tumultuous history, as we can tell from a piece of Gustavian furniture or a brine cask, say, that turns up far from its place of origin. The constant to and fro of maritime trade has helped to forge a regional identity enriched by a shared patrimony.

Today, people readily appreciate the sheer beauty of the long sandy beaches at the forest's edge and the innumerable granite islands of the archipelagos. Romantic late 19th-century villas are being restored, with their turrets, balconies and verandas, and as often as not a landing stage and matching wooden pavilion in the garden. But whether farmhouses, sailors' cottages, manor houses nestled in their vast estates or modern dwellings perfectly integrated with the natural environment, the houses of the Baltic proclaim their heritage out loud. From Denmark to Sweden, Poland, Russia, Finland or Estonia, from Germany to Lithuania or Latvia, local idiosyncrasies and common traditions are spelled out in an intricate symbiosis. In these northern lands, where the cold and the darkness are succeeded by brilliant sunshine, Midsummer's Day is the traditional occasion to celebrate the return of the fine weather – and there is much to celebrate in this unpretentious and sociable lifestyle of sailing and yacht races, fantastic fishing and long-drawn-out dinners with friends.

Russia

Icebound during the winter months, and opening on to a gulf obstructed by islands, the marshy delta of the river Neva was a particularly unpromising location. So when Peter the Great chose it as the site for his new capital, built in 1703, it was a visionary act because it offered Russia a window on to northern Europe. As a fortress it had incalculable military significance, being the key to ending Swedish hegemony in the Baltic and imposing Russian domination, and its port removed the necessity to send merchandise the long way round via Archangel. But more than that, when St Petersburg was equipped by Catherine the Great with all the civilized attractions of a capital – iconic monuments such as the Hermitage and the Winter Palace – most of them were the work of foreign artists and architects.

This 'Venice of the North' offers magnificent vistas of coloured façades ranged above its canals and bridges. Millions of tons of granite were brought in from Finland to build these grandiose schemes and to pave the streets. Despite their proximity to the town, the large islands and beautiful coastline remained unexploited until modern times.

St Petersburg became Petrograd because of anti-German feeling at the outbreak of World War I, then Leningrad to commemorate Lenin's death in 1924. However, it recovered its original name in 1991, and with it its status as a cultural capital. The celebration of the tercentenary of its foundation has served to rouse the sleeping beauty, and major works of restoration have been set in train to restore its former glory....

Between Poland and Lithuania lies another pocket of Russian territory that provides strategic access to the Baltic. It is Kaliningrad (Königsberg), former capital of East Prussia.

PAGES 10–11: The Gulf of Finland. The lights of St Petersburg can be seen from there at night.

OPPOSITE AND RIGHT: In the large park attached to Peter the Great's palace at Peterhof, Tsar Nicholas I built his summer residence, the Alexandria Cottage, on which work commenced in 1826. These photographs show one of the pavilions in the palace grounds (opposite) and outbuildings by Adam Menelaws (right).

A fashion designer and
her photographer partner
have created a studio in
a St Petersburg attic.

Some places have soul, and the studio of Larissa Pogoretskaya and Anatoly Bisinbaev is most certainly one of them. Just a stone's throw from the Marinsky Theatre, the Count's House once echoed to the sound of Anna Pavlova's ballet classes.

Eight years ago, Larissa and Anatoly moved into the top floor of a handsome Art Nouveau building, just across the road from where the poet Alexander Block once lived in the Colonna quarter, which has always been reserved for St Petersburg's artistic community. By removing the partitions that once separated the maids' rooms, they created a vast, light open space, painted white and with a wooden floor, ideal both for Larissa's workshop and Anatoly's photographic studio.

A well-known fashion designer, famous for her style of 'bohemian chic', Larissa rarely makes preliminary sketches, instead preferring to create her designs intuitively, crumpling the fabric in her hand and allowing her imagination free rein. When she has completed a collection, the models come to the studio to pose for fashion shots taken by Anatoly. As an independent artist he is working on a series of nude photographs, examples of which hang on the walls, alongside paintings by Oleg Bogomolov, Andrej Bellé and Alexander Berasimov.

Larissa and Anatoly enjoy a bohemian lifestyle and love partying. Friends often drop by unexpectedly, bottle in hand, and then the evening just takes off. A piano, guitars, drums and even a trombone are at hand for the musicians, professional or amateur, whose repertoire ranges from classical to jazz or gypsy music. They also dance to the salsa tunes that are Larissa's favourites.

Larissa and Anatoly bring back all sorts of exotic clothes from their travels abroad, which they love to wear for fancy dress evenings. All the guests – musicians, artists, journalists and diplomats – help with preparing the food. Everyone sits round a glass table, or just on the floor, plates on knees. The night is given up to talking, singing, dancing....

By her own admission, it is this intimate and vibrant atmosphere that sparks Larissa's creativity. Her childhood memories, the art books she loves to pore over, the objects she has collected on holiday – those are her other influences. Every morning when she goes to her workshop, bathed in the penetrating St Petersburg light, she looks forward to another day when the only thing to be expected is the unexpected.

PAGES 14–15: Views of the studio.

ABOVE: Displayed on the sofa are some of the hats Larissa Pogoretskaya uses to accessorize her clothes, and above them is a painting called *Lara's Dreams*, a present from Alexander Berasimov.
LEFT: Music plays an important part in this couple's life. All kinds of instruments are at their guests' disposal.
OPPOSITE: Draped on the tailor's dummy is one of Larissa's designs in progress and, on the wall, a photograph of a sexy angel by Anatoly Bisinbaev.

OVERLEAF: Views of the studio.

Opposite, Above and Right: At the upper end of the Gulf of Finland lies St Petersburg (above), the city most exposed to the icy Baltic currents. Every year it holds the record for the lowest temperatures in the region. Contradicting the principles of Palladianism, which dictate that buildings should be of an immaculate whiteness, the pastel colours of St Petersburg's neoclassical façades were designed to lend animation to the pale wintry skies and snow-covered streets (opposite and right).

Andrei Dmitriev is the
ultimate dandy, the
touchstone of elegance,
style and good taste.
His refusal to hold back or
compromise is a mark of his
passionate and expansive
Russian temperament.

Although he left St Petersburg the moment he could in order to travel the world, Andrei Dmitriev has never betrayed his city, to which he always returns. He knows by heart every single palace, and agonizes over every last 18th-century courtyard that disappears as a result of over-enthusiastic renovation. A place of exquisite sophistication submitted to a process of tragic decline, St Petersburg has taught him to appreciate the sensual pleasures of materials and perfect forms, the faded glory of a bygone age, the beauty to be found in ugliness, the nobility in poverty. As an interior decorator, his style is rooted in such incongruous juxtapositions that, all of a sudden, make blinding sense.

Because he needs solitude, Andrei permits himself the luxury of an apartment that expresses his own aesthetic tastes, adjacent to the one occupied by his family. Having undergone a recent renovation, nothing remained in it of the original 19th-century fittings. Andrei took advantage of this to remove the plaster, preferring the integrity of brick walls to any other form of camouflage. In the process a walled-up alcove was restored to his lounge, providing the perfect spot for a romantic portrait in need of a home. In the kitchen, the icon of the Virgin with Child is barely identifiable as such, denuded as it is of its coloured surface. With his background in semiology, Andrei Dmitriev likens it to a sign expressing the essence of art, a sacred presence in the course of disappearance. He spotted the icon in Moscow's flea market and did not rest until he had bought it, so scared was he that someone had walked off with it in the meantime – improbable though that may seem!

In Andrei's apartment, it is the books and objects that you notice, all chosen for their exceptional beauty and with no concern for their value, or even their original function. Thus a pasta maker has been turned into a lamp whose murky light is filtered though tiny holes. The flea market and the antique shops are his particular weakness, although he assures you that he sometimes roots through people's dustbins to find some piece of junk whose beauty has escaped its owner's notice!

When Andrei gets particularly worked up about the lack of imagination of his times, he does sometimes dream of getting away from it all, living in a palace somewhere, perhaps in Italy. But deep down he admits that wherever he might retreat to, he will always return to St Petersburg, where he is the acknowledged idol of the world of interior design.

PAGE 22: A travelling trunk, formerly in occasional use, is here pressed into full-time service.

PAGE 23 AND ABOVE: In the kitchen, collections of glass bottles and white porcelain illustrate Andrei's fascination with pure form, its lines unblurred by colour – which, for him, ought to emerge out of the natural material. There is no paint on the walls, just a curious kind of plaster that absorbs the most unlikely pigments – red wine, for example, which comes out a velvety grey. LEFT: Gilt and transparency are the order of the day in the bathroom. OPPOSITE: In the bedroom area of the loft, a brick wall reduces the pretensions of the mahogany bed.

Sweden

The most famous of the races organized by the fashionable Royal Swedish Yacht Club (KSSS) is the Gotland Runt, which takes place every year at the beginning of summer. Three hundred yachts set sail from Sandhamn on the Stockholm archipelago on a course that takes them right round the island of Gotland. The event attracts a huge following, with many spectators putting to sea in their own craft or watching from the port of Visby. The Swedish passion for sailing comes as no surprise, of course, given that mastery of the seas has been the key to their history ever since the Vikings.

Modern Sweden has managed to hang on to a number of its disputed offshore territories, among them the islands of Öland, Gotland and its tiny neighbour Fårö, which are much prized today as holiday locations. Gotland's handsome stone houses are reminders of the island's trading past, the multicoloured façades and walls of the buildings reflecting its former prosperity. In the altogether gentler climate of Sweden's southernmost region, the habitat was radically different, and the great plains of Scania were soon studded with farmsteads – not unlike the one from which naughty young Nils Holgersson is supposed to have made his escape on the back of his white gander!

These farmhouses are much in demand by today's city-dwellers who want a bolt hole in the country but love the proximity to Malmö and Copenhagen, now within easy reach since a bridge was built linking southern Sweden with Denmark. Even in Stockholm, situated as it is on an archipelago, it is possible to live by the sea and sail out to one of the islands for a few days. It could be in a 19th-century villa or an ecologically sound modern masterpiece. What people are looking for is the chance to recharge their batteries, to get back to nature and a simpler life where there is time for sunshine, hospitality and friendship.

PAGES 26–27: A view of the Stockholm archipelago.

OPPOSITE: Highly characteristic of Fårö are the ghostly shapes of limestone rocks, eaten away by the ice that envelops them in the long winter months.
RIGHT: The window of a traditional Gotland house.

A remarkable collection of old farmhouse furniture gives the seaside home of a Swedish shipowner its rustic feel.

For this Swedish shipowner, a maritime setting was pretty much a foregone conclusion. When he acquired a holiday home on the Stockholm archipelago, of course it was the sea view he was looking for. But relaxing on the veranda for a few hours watching the yachts go by was not what he had in mind: he wanted to be able to see that view from every room in the house! Walls were knocked down, and four partitioned rooms merged into a single space that opened, at ground-floor level, on to the covered veranda, from where there is an extraordinary view of the archipelago. The only thing spared was the staircase, which was left intact in its original colours.

The house has been modernized and insulated, and a proper heating system installed, making it possible to live there all year round, but it has not been furnished in a contemporary style. The owner is a great lover of Swedish antique furniture and has built up an astonishing collection over the last twenty years, scouring sale-rooms, auctions and antique shops. This acquisitive streak goes back to childhood. The lamp that hangs above the stairs, which he brought back as a small boy from a voyage to Brazil on his grandfather's yacht, bears testament to this.

The old farmhouse furniture and primitive paintings from Dalecarlia that give this house its rustic feel are now almost impossible to find. The superb Swedish wall-hangings – because they used to be taken out of the chests where they were stored all year and hung on the walls only for special occasions – have retained all the freshness of their original colours. They are their new owner's pride and joy.

Everywhere, the maritime theme crops up again: hanging in the veranda is the model of a ship, of the type once used as a votive offering in the churches of seaside villages to keep their menfolk safe from harm. There is also a copper porthole converted into a mirror and, on every wall, amateur paintings of ships by sailors, immensely touching in their painstaking concern to render every last detail. You hazard a guess that our shipowner, marooned on dry land, wants a constant reminder of the freedom he associates with life at sea.

PAGE 30: One of the small guest houses, seen from the small terrace outside the front door.

ABOVE AND OPPOSITE: At one time, the lives of the inhabitants of these coastal regions revolved around sailing and boatbuilding. Models of ships, similar to the one on the veranda (opposite) and sometimes of threatening proportions, were hung from church roofs; prayers inscribed on the hull asked for divine protection against bad weather, the perils of war or piracy. These models are now collector's items, much sought after by sailing enthusiasts, shipowners, yachtsmen and amateur sailors. The paintings of sailing ships (above) were done by sailors to pass the time on long voyages.

OPPOSITE AND ABOVE: With its footrest raised above the cold floor, the kitchen table (opposite) offers a splendid illustration of sound peasant common sense. An element of colour is injected by the painted motifs of vases and garlands on the wooden corner cupboards (in the kitchen, and above in the drawing room), which are a rustic variant of the rococo style in vogue in the 18th century.

Examples of this naive style of decoration are now highly desirable. They were drawn freehand and in situ by itinerant painters who brought to the provinces the fashions prevailing at court.

RIGHT: Displayed in a frame hanging by the fireside is a typical Dalecarlia painting, its charming little figures defying the logic of scale or realism.

'On one of the islands he saw a big white castle and, just to the east of it, the shore began to fill up with villas of every style, widely spaced at first and then increasingly close together. Here was a small castle, there a house in miniature. Over there a long single-storey manor house had been built, there a villa complete with turrets. Some of these stood in their own gardens, but the majority were scattered about the woods covering the banks.

And yet, whatever the differences between them, they had one thing in common, which is that they were not sober and serious like other buildings but attractively painted in bright colours, green, blue, white and red, like play huts.'

Selma Lagerlöf, *The Wonderful Adventures of Nils Holgersson*

On the island of Fårö,
living close to nature
means committing yourself
to the use of natural
materials: weathered wood,
white lead, sheepskin....

Helen Müller returns from long walks by the sea with her pockets filled with the pebbles of lightweight white chalk that wink up at you from the path; but what she would really like to do is bring the whole of Fårö back with her and take it to Stockholm, cling on as long as possible to the intense happiness she feels on the island and be able to share it with friends.

Helen quite simply fell head over heels in love with this little island close to Gotland, which was introduced to her by her husband Marcus who had spent every summer there since he was a child. Flat, arid and sandy, Fårö is dominated by its skies of intense luminosity and colour. This is the island to go to for replenishing one's reserves, the place where Helen just lets nature wash over her and absorbs its energies. It is a lesson learned long ago by Ingmar Bergman, who shot a number of his films here before making the island his permanent home.

Fårö is known as Sheep Island and has a large animal population. The binoculars hanging by the front door are used by parents and children alike to study the many different species of birds. Their greatest delight, however, is watching the antics of the neighbours' ponies, and they love trips out to sea in their sailing boat, which spends its winters hull in the air, upside down on the beach.

Respecting an environment in such a remarkable state of preservation was a sine qua non: it was essential that the house should simply melt into the protected landscape. Helen and Marcus's solution was to approach an architect friend, Thomas Nathorst-Böös, and ask him to design a wooden house. With its grey patination and steeply sloping roofs, it looks barely any different from the old farmhouses in the vicinity, and gives the impression it has always been there.

Inside, there is a large modern space, white and bright. It is a flexible open area where everyone foregathers: children, friends, the friends of the children, the children of friends, all part of that whole freewheeling holiday experience. In furnishing the house, Helen looked to the craftsmen of Gotland. It is something very special about the islands, she thinks, that the obligation to use local resources has encouraged craftsmen who produce original quality work. The birch chairs, for example, are white-leaded and oiled, with sheepskin cushions – an island speciality, and one she loves because it is so soft and comfortable.

Along with the pebbles she collects compulsively, Helen takes back to Stockholm at the end of every summer a number of objects and pieces of furniture made in Gotland. That way she can continue to enjoy the delights of the Swedish islands throughout the rest of the year, and share them with the clients of her interior design shop.

PAGES 38–39: Inspired by the local wooden farmhouses, Helen and Marcus's house differs only in respect of its large windows, which are designed to let in as much light as possible.

OPPOSITE: When the wind whistles or the winter is too severe, everyone huddles round the hearth. On the mantelshelf are displayed pieces of ceramic, pebbles and driftwood from the beach (detail above), all of local origin!

RIGHT: Sheepskin – which keeps Swedish babies snug in their straw baskets – is used here to make seat covers for the dining chairs (bottom right), while a stool found in Dalecarlia (top right) is covered in cowhide.

ABOVE AND OPPOSITE: A beautiful light and airy open space – that was the ultimate goal to be kept in mind during the construction of the house, which was designed in close cooperation with an architect friend. Gone are the days of tiny kitchens relegated to the end of a corridor behind closed doors. The large open-plan kitchen (opposite) is simple and functional and ideal for socializing. The bathroom (above) required a bit more in the way of privacy and was therefore provided with a door.

OVERLEAF: The wild, rugged shoreline of Fårö.

This handsome white early 20th-century villa on the Stockholm archipelago is redolent with period charm, as haunting as the scent of roses....

Three children in sailor suits occupy the white boat being steered by a young man through the waters of the Stockholm archipelago. The family photograph perfectly captures the elegance and carefree atmosphere of Sweden before the outbreak of World War I. In 1912, Erik Hirsch, who made his fortune by inventing the milk separator, had a villa built on the small island of Stegesund, designed by Ivar Tengbom. At the time, he had of course no idea that his young architect was to become a leading practitioner of the art in the 1920s, famous for his stripped-down classical style.

Hirsch's house is in fact representative of the prevailing Art Nouveau of which Tengbom, an avid devourer of the English periodical *The Studio*, was particularly enamoured at the time. Granted, the handsome fluted Doric columns flanking the main entrance and supporting the porch do anticipate the classical style the architect subsequently developed, but the sloping roofs and organic outlines of the house are the living proof of his perfect mastery of Art Nouveau. The spacious white interior, logically distributed around the staircase, corresponds to the principles of clarity and simplicity laid down by Viollet-le-Duc and John Ruskin. White furniture and Liberty wallpaper complete the look, with the addition of a few Biedermeier touches. It is all very much in the spirit of Sundborn, home of the painter Carl Larsson – which was familiar to the whole of Sweden via his delightful watercolours – but transformed by the subtlety of the detailing.

Nothing much has altered since the grandfather's day, except perhaps the steamboats that once served the islands. In the garden arbours, you almost think you catch sight of elegant women from the early 20th century sipping their tea out of Swedish china from Rörstrand.... For the moment the summer term ended, the Hirsch family would ensconce themselves in their summer quarters at Solgård (Sun House), taking along all the staff and condemning papa to commute to and fro from Stockholm. A farm supplied the kitchens with meat and eggs, while the greenhouse and the vegetable garden provided all the fruit and vegetables needed for island life. Today the grandson of Erik Hirsch, Per Wästberg, is a member of the Swedish Academy, and he has appointed himself the chronicler of this summer paradise as his grandfather experienced it during the thirties. He describes the passion with which they all took up sailing and participated in the excessively smart regattas organized by the Royal Swedish Yacht Club (KSSS). The family album contains photos of Erik Hirsch having coffee on his yacht, *Ta-Ta*, surrounded by members of the crew. Amusing also to imagine the gentlemen out on the porch smoking a cigar after dinner, while the ladies perched on cane chairs, enveloped in their shawls.

Time has not stood still at Solgård, where the sound of children's laughter is perhaps more common today than it was in the past. Yet the garden is still full of roses and the Rörstrand china is still brought out at teatime. New generations take up sailing, and the pages of the family album fill up with images of present happiness.

ABOVE AND RIGHT: One of Solgård's most striking features is the sense of unity that prevails throughout. Because Ivar Tengbom, its architect, was inspired by the Arts and Crafts Movement, he viewed the house as a totality: the sideboard in the dining room (above) and mirrored wardrobe in the bedroom (right) were designed specifically to match the style of architecture. Proportions, materials for furniture, fabrics and wallpaper are all in perfect harmony. One survivor from the Gustavian age is the Swedish stove (above) which calls to mind the blue and white china of the Rörstrand factory.

PAGES 46–47 AND OVERLEAF: Idyllic views from the bedrooms over the Stockholm archipelago.

Every house in Gotland contains some small treasure from the island's Viking past.

Anders Palmér is an artist, more specifically a landscape painter, who for some twenty years now has found his inspiration on the island of Gotland. As his paintings are often of very large proportions, he does not use an easel but paints on to a flat canvas unrolled directly on the stony ground. The titles of his works are like an invitation to his collectors to come to Gotland and see for themselves. It was a girlfriend who originally brought him to spend a holiday on the island, then unknown to him as he had always spent the summer at the family home in Skåne (Scania). He began to dream about having a house there where he could go to paint for half the year. In the event his wish was granted as the result of a complete coincidence, when a friend took him along to pick up the keys of a house he was renting on the island. It just so happened that the house next door was for sale, and Anders made up his mind then and there: although he had barely even seen it, this was the house for him.

Renovating the building, which for a long time had only been used for storage, took him ten years. In reinforcing the walls, traces of the original colours were revealed, including a façade of a reddish ochre that matched the setting sun. One of Anders's great pleasures is to pass the long summer evenings on the terrace that has been created inside the stone walls of what was once a kitchen.

The house is not large: just an entrance hall, a kitchen and two rooms. Our painter therefore decided to make himself a bedroom under the eaves, retaining the bare stone walls. The ground-floor rooms were repainted in the colours they had originally boasted three hundred years ago, a time when the use of such pigments was a mark of wealth. Wall alcoves once used for storing food are now the home for books and decorative objects. But Anders has really not changed very much else, as the last thing he wanted was to introduce into a 17th/18th-century house the sort of modernity he feels at home with in Stockholm. Instead he has managed to track down copies of the furniture at Gripsholm Castle, a style he regards as much more in keeping with the decor of the Gotland house.

History is all around you on this peaceful Baltic island. Up to the time of the Danish invasion, before the German traders brought prosperity to its capital of Visby, Gotland was the fiefdom of the Vikings. Chance archaeological finds are commonplace on the island and Anders's neighbours proudly display rusty old nails, keys and knives. He himself likes to speculate on the treasures that still lie hidden from prying eyes, for his house was built on the estate known as Hägvards, in the north-west of the island, and stands on the foundations of an old Viking farm. Echoes of this ancient and mythic past may be deciphered in the Gotland painter's works.

ABOVE: Gotland is the southernmost of the Swedish provinces and the one where the sun shines longest – hence perhaps the rather Provençal feel of the terrace. It is the site for many a delightful evening as the collapsed stonework of the former kitchen retains the heat of the day. Beyond it lies a garden which provides all the aromatic herbs needed for the kitchen. Anders believes his recent passion for Tuscany, where he currently teaches and paints for half the year, has its roots in these summers spent on the Swedish island.

OPPOSITE: In the bedroom built under the eaves, the stone walls have been left in their original condition.

Pages 56–57: The sitting room.

Opposite and Right: The blue sitting room (opposite) dates from the 17th century and is part of the original house, although the traces of a fresco on the wall above the fireplace are of more recent origin. To the left is an alcove, today used purely for display purposes but once a place to store jams at a constant temperature. The dining room (top right) occupies an 18th-century extension. If you add to this the entrance hall, red with a simple band of grey, and the kitchen in almond green (bottom right), all of Gotland's traditional colours are represented. The attractive odd set of blue and white crockery was sought out item by item in second-hand shops and salerooms.

ABOVE AND LEFT: The island of Gotland has as many sheep as it does human inhabitants! The dry, rocky soil of the Baltic islands makes agriculture difficult but the heathland provides the flocks with huge pastures, their boundaries marked by dry-stone walls made of the characteristic Gotland limestone (left).

OPPOSITE (TOP): Bunches of flax hung out to dry on a wooden frame, ready to be woven during the winter months.

OPPOSITE (BOTTOM): Nineteenth-century wooden houses and German-influenced half-timbered farmhouses make up the island's housing stock.

For Eva Darpö, Gotland
is a reminder of her
grandmother and the
source of inspiration
for her work as an artist.

It is called Spring House, *Gaustäde* in Gotland's curious Swedish dialect, with its admixture of Danish, German and even Russian – a vivid illustration in itself of the way this island at the heart of the Baltic was fought over by the coastal powers in the age of the Vikings and under the Hanseatic League. Since 1645, the island has belonged to Sweden, and this limestone house with its tiled roof dates all the way back to that period of the 17th century when wood was kept solely for shipbuilding, and there would have been no question of putting up a wooden house or even of panelling its interior. The solid stone walls of Gaustäde were therefore painted in bright colours: blue picked out in red for the outside door and window apertures, and yellow, red and green in combination with grey-blue for the interiors. Ultramarine and cobalt blue were particularly favoured, especially for kitchens, where they were thought to deter flies. Over the last six years, all the rooms at Gaustäde have been restored to their original colours, thanks to work undertaken in part by the Commission for Historic Monuments and in part by Eva's father. Everything has been done by the book, using natural pigments mixed with oil and egg.

Not that this was the first house Eva's father had done up. A former funeral mason, it was something he had been used to doing all his life. When he was a young man, he met his future wife on Gotland, and the two of them determined to return there when they retired. Now it is on his daughter's behalf that he has been slaving away, first finding and then restoring the house, and tracking down furniture on the island.

Eva used to spend her summers as a child on the neighbouring small island of Fårö in her grandmother's old windmill, which consisted of round rooms on a number of levels. What she wanted for herself was a space where she could still spend the holidays with her family but also have somewhere to work with glass and ceramics, and to exhibit. With its outbuildings, Gaustäde in the small village of Fårösund, in the north of the island, fulfilled all her requirements. The main house was used as the living space, while Eva installed her studio in what was once the forge and transformed the stables into a gallery, where she exhibits her sculptures every summer alongside paintings by various friends, among them Anders Palmér.

Although she would be hard pressed to say exactly how, the island of Gotland has a strong influence on her work. It may be the penetrating summer light, the arid heathland dominated by heavy skies, or the greyish tinge that clings to all the colours – Eva finds it impossible to say. The flash of the waves and the luminosity of the first white flowers of summer never cease to amaze her. Or, who knows, it may just conceivably be something in the water…. Could it be from the spring at Gaustäde that she draws her inspiration?

PAGES 64–65: The small dining room.

ABOVE AND RIGHT: On a rococo chair are some of the glasses made by Eva Darpö in her workshop. She also uses the furnace to make her wonderfully insubstantial sculptures of birds. OPPOSITE: Great care went into the restoration of the wall decorations in the formal dining room (in the foreground), which consist of a painted frieze running along the top of the wall and a broad band of grey at the base, in the manner of a plinth. The original flooring had been used for firewood, so it was replaced with antiqued wooden boards, often left bare, as in the small dining room (pages 64–65). In the other rooms, as in most northern interiors, woven rag runners protect the floors.

OPPOSITE AND ABOVE: Eva is sensitive
to the house's particular atmosphere
and takes care that everything in the
way of decorative objects and
furniture is old, whether it belonged
to her grandmother or was spotted
on the island or brought in from one
of the other Swedish provinces –
as is the case with the wooden
bench covered in sheepskin
(opposite, in the kitchen). In the
country that was where people used
to sleep in preference to using a
proper bed; some were even made
with an extension that could be
folded away during the day.

The 17th-century paving stones
in the kitchen are virtually unscathed.
In the back kitchen (above), a chest
covered by a woollen tapestry is set
in front of the open fire once used
both for heating this part of the house
and for cooking.

OVERLEAF: Boathouses on the Fårö
shore.

The story starts
with a rococo sofa.
Nothing so unusual about
that perhaps, and yet....

Barbro Grandelius was living in Dalecarlia in central Sweden when her husband Göran Peterson returned home from an auction with a Gustavian sofa.... For Barbro, a ceramicist and a big fan of Pop Art, this sofa was to change everything. She was sufficiently intrigued to find out more about the style (the expression of 18th-century Swedish neoclassicism during the reign of Gustav III, r. 1771–92) and when they moved to Skåne, where this type of furniture was freely available, it became a real passion. One find led to the next, and in no time she found herself the proud owner of a collection, which completely swamped the seventies style of their place in Malmö. Moulded white china, teapots, candlesticks and soup tureens of great beauty and simplicity became her passions. It was not long before it became clear that the sofa would appear to greater advantage in a period setting.

Göran and Barbro looked all over Skåne and two years ago, on the eve of Göran's fiftieth birthday, they found the house of their dreams. It was a small manor house dating from the early 19th century that had once belonged to a Baltic German called Gosselman. The house was near the delightful village of Ystad which has many ancient buildings – among them a 12th-century church, an 18th-century manor house and a 17th-century inn. Just four kilometres away is the Baltic Sea, with its beautiful wild beaches.

Set in a large garden that had been restored to its original appearance a few years before, the house was even more lovely inside than they had dared to hope. On two floors, linked by a handsome staircase, the original layout had been preserved, as had a magnificent tiled stove and the tall windows with their internal shutters. Barbro started to scratch off the layers of paint in the hope of discovering the original colour of the walls but was forced to admit that they had been covered with wall hangings, as the little holes left by tapestry pins tended to confirm. Only the wooden doors revealed traces of colour where they had been picked out here and there in grey. The floor had suffered from years of neglect and had to be relaid with broad pine planks, while the walls were repainted in pale grey and white. The Gustavian furniture soon took its place in the refurbished manor house and was complemented by four overdoors with grisaille decorations of garlands, acquired when a castle and its contents were put on the market.

Unable to carry on accumulating all her impulse buys, Barbro has also opened a shop, putting up for sale the Gustavian pieces which she now travels all over Sweden to find. Delighted to share her passion with other people and to take advantage of the lovely surroundings into which she has put so much of herself, Barbro also has plans to hold musical evenings and lectures in her home, rather in the manner of an 18th-century salon. The Gosselman manor house is a beautiful piece of restoration, which subtly recreates the simplicity of the past. It will be a delight to see it spring to life on one of these evenings, by the light of its crystal chandelier.

ABOVE AND OPPOSITE: Barbro's taste
is for plain pieces with simple shapes
(pages 72–73 and opposite). Colour is
used sparingly, just the predominant
white and grey of the Gustavian
furniture; nothing jarring, utterly
simple materials, notably china,
cotton and wood, whether left bare
or painted, in a setting of restrained
elegance. The bathroom, for
example, has been painted white
but one of the walls is bare wood
(above). The only object in the least
bit ornate is the sparkling crystal
chandelier hanging in the small
lounge (opposite), which helps
create a warm, stylish atmosphere
for musical gatherings.
LEFT: The garden setting.

PAGES 76–77: The bedroom features an original tiled stove.

ABOVE AND OPPOSITE: When Barbro scours the antique shops, she tries to distinguish between the pieces she wants to keep and things she will sell on. But it never pays to be too sentimental, and the famous rococo sofa that started off the whole crazy adventure was actually sold last spring and replaced with a large bench-style sofa with simple jute cushions (opposite).

As in most Nordic houses, the windows are curtainless. The internal shutters in the salon are original.

Elisabeth Holte opens the door of her house, lets the cats in and perches on the step to look out over the plain stretching before her to the horizon. Here she can draw a deep breath and forget the kilometres she has covered on the journey from Norway to this part of the Swedish countryside on the southernmost tip of Skåne. Elisabeth bought the house when she was the Stockholm correspondent for a Norwegian daily newspaper. She had long wanted a home of her own, and found exactly what she wanted with the help of a lawyer in Skåne. The Norwegians speak of this region in the same breath as Tuscany because of the sweetness of the landscape: fields of blue flax in spring and yellow rape in summer, sheep, and long sandy beaches on the Baltic that have no counterpart in Norway. Once night has come, when the plain is plunged into darkness and the lights of the farmhouses twinkle in the distance, like the lights of ships that are strangely becalmed, Elisabeth has the sensation of being out on the open sea. What could be more attractive than to light the candles of the gilded chandelier suspended from the branches of her magnificent oak tree and pass some time with her friends, nearby farmers and the artists and antique dealers who have come in their numbers to set up home in Skåne. This is a place where the peace of the country and a cultural life go hand in hand: one day out in the fields, the next at a private view in Simrishamn or Ystad.

The biggest compliment you can pay her is to assume, quite sincerely, that the house is older than it really is, so successfully has Elisabeth recreated the character of a local farmhouse. Little more than an empty shell, it had provided a modest home for two peasant families since it was built in 1917. Although it had to be renovated from top to bottom, not a sign of the work remains. The small whitewashed farmhouse with a slate roof was extended to take in the old barn that lay at right angles to the dwelling house. With the four original rooms plus three new ones, Elisabeth has space for the treasures brought back from her travels all over the world, many of these authentic peasant pieces picked up for a song. She has given the interior warmth and interest by using old mattress ticking with red stripes for cushion covers, while terracotta egg plates (used for chopped bacon omelettes with blueberry jam) serve as her everyday crockery. Digging around in antique and second-hand shops is one of her hobbies, and her eagle eye is capable of spotting amazing finds tucked away at the bottom of some old peasant chest.

Daydreaming, strolling over the vast beaches nearby, walking to the lighthouse at Sandhammaren, that is how she spends most of her time when she is far removed from the stresses and strains of the town and the full diary that goes with her job as editor of a Norwegian interior decoration magazine. Before she leaves, Elisabeth casts one last look round the small courtyard, which is paved with pebbles dug up out of the fields during the building work, and it seems to sum up everything that draws her back.

It was no more than an empty shell set in beautiful countryside when a Norwegian journalist set about turning it into a proper home that reflected her own taste and enthusiasms.

Pages 80–81: The garden opens directly on to the Skåne plain.

Opposite and Above: Linking the barn with the living quarters of this former farmstead has enabled Elisabeth Holte to create a number of new rooms. The old part of the house now comprises an entrance hall, a kitchen (opposite, in the background) and a dressing room (above). From the entrance hall (opposite, foreground), the floor of which is painted in black and white squares like a chessboard, a wooden staircase leads up to Elisabeth's summer bedroom under the roof.

ABOVE: The wooden bench in the kitchen was bought in Manhattan in the 1970s and originates from the south-west of France. It arrived here by convoluted means, including a brief spell in some stables belonging to Jackie Onassis.

RIGHT: Today purely decorative, the china eggs filling this earthenware crock once had quite another function: placed inside nesting boxes, they were meant to encourage the hens to lay.

OPPOSITE: On the wooden bench in the guest room, the cushions are covered with linen and cotton mattress ticking and woollen bedcovers; the red-striped fabrics lend a touch of warmth and cheer to the room. Similar fabric is used for the bedclothes on the copper bedstead that is partly visible on the far right.

Opposite and Above: Elisabeth has installed her summer bedroom under the eaves and enjoys a magnificent view across the plain. It has a very stripped-down feel, with simple furniture of bare wood, rough antique linen sheeting and authentic woollen blankets. At the other end of the attic is a second bed, also with covers made from mattress ticking.

Denmark

Denmark owes its wealth and influence to the strategic position it occupies between the Baltic and the North Sea. Although most of its territory lies on the Jutland peninsula, the establishment of the capital at Copenhagen, on one of the 406 islands, reflects the crucial importance of its straits – passage through which was made subject to a royal tax as far back as 1429. So vital was the narrow route off Elsinore that the proceeds from the so-called Sound Duty enabled Denmark to dominate mercantile traffic in the Baltic right up to the 18th century.

The Danish kings at first extended their conquests out to the west – where in the early part of the 11th century they founded an Anglo-Danish empire – and then at the end of the 12th century towards Estonia and Courland. In 1397, the Union of Kalmar brought all the Scandinavian kingdoms under their dominion. When the Danes lost Sweden in the 16th century, the inhabitants of the island of Bornholm refused to submit to their new masters; they took the Swedish Lieutenant-Governor prisoner and killed him when he tried to escape. A delegation went to Copenhagen to swear allegiance to the Danish King.

At the heart of the Baltic, Bornholm offers two contrasting types of landscape. The north, with its eroded rocky coastline, has a Scandinavian character, while the sandy shores in the south are typical of the beautiful beaches on the Baltic mainland. The most wooded of all Denmark's provinces, the island is also famous for its traditional herring smokehouses and windmills.

PAGES 90–91: Farms strung out over the undulating plain on Bornholm's eastern side.

OPPOSITE AND RIGHT: Wheat and oats are Bornholm's main crops, and the island has deposits of kaolin clay, used locally in the manufacture of ceramics.

Do you need to be born in the Baltic to live there on an island all year round? Or is it some mad desire for freedom that makes the isolation so appealing?

Finn is a sea captain, and when he goes to sea, Jette Iversen never forgets to turn the two little china dogs that stand in the window to face the road, so they can wait there faithfully for their master's return. In so doing she is carrying on the ritual inherited from her grandmother, also a captain's wife on Bornholm. For Jette, who had left Bornholm, returning to the island where she was born was for a long time a distant dream, but one she was finally able to realize in 1979 when she bought a house in Salmon Street in Rønne, the island's principal town. A few years later, Finn moved into the house across the road. When the pair decided to live together, they kept both houses so that family and friends could come and stay in the holidays.

Though built in 1830 and 1850 respectively, the two houses are identical, long and low, distinguished only by a half-timbered rear façade to the older building. In one of the gardens where Jette lovingly tends her flowers and vegetable plot, the mild climate has allowed her to grow a vine and even a magnificent fig tree.

When she moved back to the island of Bornholm, Jette bought nothing. She was content either to recycle or design the furniture she needed. In her parents' home, for example, she found an unfinished wooden bench her father had intended to give her mother before they were married. She put all the pieces back together and painted it black. The portraits of her grandparents hanging on the wall are the record of her family history, and also the symbol of her personal stake in the island. In Finn's house, Jette has preferred to use modern furniture, and she has chosen the best Denmark has to offer: Arne Jacobsen. No more than a minute away from each other, as far as everyday living is concerned the two houses function as one, with each retaining its own particular atmosphere and traditions.

'A Bornholmer,' explains Jette with a laugh, 'is an inhabitant of Bornholm, a pendulum clock and a smoked herring!' A Bornholmer all year round, Jette enjoys her houses and gardens, with their views of windmills and the tall white chimneys of the fish smokehouses. Even if she sometimes feels the need to leap on the boat and go to Copenhagen to breathe the air of the capital, on the island she has a very strong sense of her identity as an island-dweller. This is home, her own little bit of happiness.

PAGE 94: A view of the entrance hall in Finn's house.

ABOVE AND RIGHT: On Bornholm, the traditional method of construction is half-timbering according to the German model. Because of the many windows that punctuate their façades, the houses in Salmon Street (above) – the prettiest in town – benefit from natural light all day long. Ecological correctness dictates the use of bicycles (right).

OPPOSITE: Ceramics, textiles and glassblowing are among Bornholm's traditional crafts. Before becoming an architect, Jette learned the technique of glassblowing, although her interest is now confined to the collection of antique glass that occupies the windowsills, the ideal location to show off the iridescent transparency of decanters, goblets and flagons.

ABOVE AND RIGHT: The island of Bornholm is Denmark's most wooded province and Almindigen, at the heart of the island, is the country's second largest forest. When Jette's father retired, he became an enthusiastic wood-turner, producing plates, bowls, cups and eggs for his daughter.

OPPOSITE: In the kitchen, an ironmonger's cabinet discovered in Copenhagen has been converted into a work surface. Children are fascinated by its many drawers and delight in speculating about the items they once contained.

OPPOSITE: The table was designed
by Piet Hein and Bruno Mathsson,
and a light fitting by Louis Poulsen
completes the look. With their
bold, clean lines, these pieces have
become classics of modern interior
design, and they fit perfectly into the
period dwelling.

The restoration of Finn's house
has been an ongoing project over
the last ten years. There have been
a number of restrictions, all to do
with authenticity – the need to use
traditional materials, for example, and
respect for local custom in the case
of windows.

ABOVE: Not spacious, Bornholm's
houses have an intimate charm.
Tucked under the roof, the attic room
looks a little like a nomad's tent,
opening on to a starry sky.

Germany

While Rügen's towering cliffs cannot fail to conjure up the romantic landscapes of Caspar David Friedrich, the jagged coastline and deserted beaches of Germany's Baltic shore are now beginning to develop their own sort of period charm, as they benefit from that 'Ostalgia' or nostalgia for East Germany much talked of since reunification. Yet, historically, this is a dynamic region, for it is the epicentre of German trade. In the 13th century, it was merchants from Lübeck who set out from these shores and established the route linking London with Novgorod, and who pursued their activities in the various towns around the Baltic founded by the Teutonic Knights and the Swordbrothers. It was because of the influence of these German traders that Low German was adopted as the common language and brick was used for the construction of the new town centres: houses with attics and storerooms, the town hall on the marketplace, the guildhalls that were the symbols of their power, and the vast churches-cum-halls.

Even the decline of the Hanseatic League in the 17th century and the liquidation of its assets in 1862 did not mean the disappearance of the German merchants, who in practice gave a new impetus to trade against the backdrop of the Industrial Revolution. And it was these same prosperous citizens who, because they appreciated the sea for its healthgiving properties, were happy to adopt the new lifestyle recommended by doctors – leisure no longer being regarded as the sole prerogative of the aristocracy but accessible also to the bourgeoisie – and build themselves seaside villas, which they would open up as soon as the fine weather arrived. Thus the modern ritual of the seaside holiday was born.

PAGES 102–103: Wicker beach chairs at Travemünde, with their backs turned against the prevailing wind.

OPPOSITE AND RIGHT: The seaside resort of Travemünde, in the bay of Lübeck, has a direct train link with St Petersburg. It was one of the tsars' favourite holiday retreats.

Thomas Mann called it
'Lübeck's prettiest
daughter', and the holiday
resort of Travemünde lives
up to that description.

The house that now belongs to Barbara and Torge Karlsruhen was used as a holiday home by a family who lived in Hamburg in the 1900s, and it transports you right back to the days when Travemünde was blossoming into an elegant and sophisticated seaside resort. When the new owners left Berlin ten years ago to move to Lübeck's outer port on the mouth of the Trave, their intention was to start a new life that was the exact opposite of that led by all their neighbours. Their idea was to live by the sea all year round and return to Berlin for the holidays.

A man with an academic background who spends his days poring over his writing, Torge appreciates the peacefulness of his workroom in the vast attic space with its sweeping views over the sea. Barbara takes advantage of the sunny mornings to walk on the beach before tackling the day's chores and tending her garden. Predominantly white and green, enlivened by the blue of hydrangeas and the pink of rhododendrons, it represents her reward for the long hours spent getting it back into shape.

If Barbara and Torge love their new life far removed from the urban grind, it is in part because they are able to participate in local cultural activities. Only one hour from Hamburg and three from Copenhagen, Travemünde's location is its trump card. Torge likes to go sailing on the Baltic, and not a week passes when he does not drive to Hamburg or Schwerin, former capital of the Dukes of Mecklenburg whose names figure so heavily in Swedish history. Yet not so very long ago Schwerin was completely inaccessible because it was in East Germany – so near and yet so far. The border between the two Germanys actually crossed the beach at Travemünde, just a few hundred metres from the house. In the East, it was forbidden to use the beach or swim: it would have been so easy to take just a few more strokes and end up on the other side of the Iron Curtain.

Going to opening nights in the theatres of Hamburg and Schwerin is one of Torge's highly agreeable duties as a drama critic. But for their two daughters, one of whom lives in England and the other in the United States, it is Travemünde's calm and restful way of life that they particularly appreciate when they come for holidays. A guest house has been installed in the garden especially for them, so that everyone can do as they please on the frequent occasions when the family gathers together.

PAGES 106–107 AND ABOVE: Since
Barbara and her husband became
the owners of a house by the sea,
she has discovered a passion for
antiques. The classical mirrors,
chandeliers and candlesticks that
she likes to collect blend perfectly
with the more modern furniture.
RIGHT: Three pairs of Danish
gardening clogs owned by Barbara.
OPPOSITE: In the salon, metal
chairs by Harry Bertoia are perfectly
at home with a clock that dates from
the late 18th century, which Barbara
and her husband brought back in
their yacht after a trip along the
Swedish coast.

OPPOSITE AND ABOVE: Lübeck's brick
buildings are typical of those in
the other maritime towns of the
Hanseatic League. The circular
apertures pierced in the walls of the
fortress enclosing the Marienkirche
(above) and in the façade of the town
hall (opposite) are a means of denying
a purchase to the wind that whistles
through the town.

In a residential area of Lübeck, the house of a collector of contemporary art.

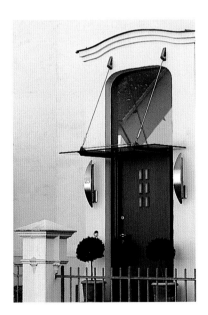

Hot countries have little appeal and if he takes a holiday abroad it is to go skiing in St Moritz or Zermatt. In the summer, like the majority of the residents of northern Europe, Dr Marwitz prefers to stay at home in Lübeck, taking advantage of the sunny hinterland and going off on his parents' boat to explore Scandinavia. He reckons that he knows the coasts of Denmark and Sweden by heart.

Dr Marwitz originally moved from Hamburg to Lübeck to set up a dental practice and he immediately succumbed to the charms of the former Queen of the Hanseatic League, beloved of Thomas Mann, Edvard Munch and Günter Grass. He also loves the proximity of the beach at Travemünde. And being able to walk everywhere, or ride his bicycle for longer excursions, encountering familiar faces on his way to work, gives him a lifestyle that suits him down to the ground. If he is absolutely desperate to go to a concert or a museum or a theatre, then Hamburg is only an hour away and offers him all the choice he could wish for.

Ensconced in a pleasant apartment in the Old Town, he would no doubt have stayed put were it not that the art was beginning to take over – not only was there more of it, but the individual pieces were growing in size. For Dr Marwitz is also a collector, with a bias towards minimalist sculpture and paintings with simple, powerful forms. He does not go to galleries on the whole, but likes to get to know the individual artists, watch them at work and see them develop over time. Rather than spread himself and buy lots of pieces by unknown artists, he prefers to concentrate on just a few whose work he likes and follow their careers, often becoming a personal friend in the process. Axel Cassel, Jean Zuber, Dietz Eilbacher and Irmer are part of his 'stable', all of whom work in the particular vein that he favours.

It was in a residential quarter near the Trave that our dentist's choice lit on a house built in 1901, which offered him all the space and light he was looking for. His architect suggested building a roof terrace that would be invisible from the street, and now he likes nothing more than to enjoy his aperitif up there in the evening as he contemplates the town of Lübeck below him; comfortably installed in a high-backed wicker armchair of the type you see on the Baltic beaches, he is even sheltered from the wind.

Whether it is having friends round or inviting one of his artists to stay – Dietz Eilbacher has just completed a new piece for the garden – Dr Marwitz likes to entertain, a purpose for which his house is ideal. He is a happy man. When you hear him enumerating the region's attractions, you discover that he is also a keen golfer. He cannot believe his luck that the course is right next to the sea, allowing him to enjoy the beauty of the coast as he plays....

PAGE 112: The wicker beach chair on the roof terrace is the ideal spot to soak up the summer sun.

ABOVE AND OPPOSITE: It was the large canvases by Jean Zuber (above, in the drawing room) that made Dr Marwitz decide to move to a much bigger space where the paintings could be properly displayed. Having been introduced to the Swiss painter in Paris by Axel Cassel, Dr Marwitz has consistently followed the progress of his work and regularly added to his collection.

The five stories and high ceilings of his new home mean that he can surround himself with massive pieces such as the monumental monolithic sculpture by Dietz Eilbacher in the drawing room (opposite). The furniture too, which includes a chair by Jean Prouvé (above), is chosen for its sculptural qualities.

OPPOSITE AND ABOVE: It was sheer chance that brought about Dr Marwitz's association with German sculptor Alex Cassel, whose sister happened to be one of his patients. Knowing of her dentist's tastes as a collector, she showed him some of her brother's exhibition catalogues.

He was immediately so taken with what he saw that he went straight to see Cassel in Normandy, and bought his first piece – an elongated human figure that reminded him of totemic figures he had come across in the course of travels overseas (above). A friendship sprang up between the two men, punctuated by meetings and further acquisitions (opposite).

Dr Marwitz particularly enjoys the different views of his artworks afforded by the maze of stairways and corridors.

OPPOSITE: Twice a year, the collector holds a big party for up to fifty people, which is the opportunity for him to show off his latest passions. A sculpture by Cassel stands outside the dining room, in which it is possible to see a rocket-shaped sculpture by Irmer on the wall.

ABOVE: On the top floor, below the roof terrace, other sculptures by Alex Cassel have found their home in Dr Marwitz's vast bedroom. A sliding glass door leads to the en-suite bathroom.

RIGHT: The library contains a fine selection of art books, as well as a reclining chair by Le Corbusier.

Painted white, bright
blue and black, a barge
moored on the island
of Hiddensee is an
invitation to laze away
the days under the wide
open skies of Pomerania.

Young Erik Krettek is just sixteen years old. He spends all his summers on the barge bought by his family eleven years ago in Potsdam. It is called *The Patriot*, a name that conjures up Germany's military past. Given its dilapidated state when they purchased it, architect Steffi Weihrauch and her husband Udo Krettek, a former engineer, had to call on all their skills to restore it to its original glory bit by bit and repair the few furnishings that remained.

To accommodate both Erik's family and his uncle's, five bedrooms were needed, as well as a bathroom, kitchen, DIY space and, most important, several reception rooms, allowing space for everyone to relax in their own way – although actually the best moments of all tend to be those spent out on the deck, just letting time pass by. Lacking a motor, the barge is permanently moored, but no matter – Erik can still get out his rod or skim stones without leaving home. But as it would be just too cruel to be at sea without going anywhere, a small motorboat is available for trips in the Baltic and for Erik to go fishing with his father.

Getting *The Patriot* to Hiddensee was a major performance as it had to be towed along every river lying between Potsdam and the Baltic. Fortunately, making the trip to Rostock for the five-yearly refurbishment is not so difficult. Normally, when you come to Hiddensee by road from Berlin, you have to leave the car on the mainland and catch a ferry out to the island. In winter, though, when you come to check the barge is in good shape, you can drive right up to it over the frozen ice. And what a delight it is in summer to live on an island where there are no cars, so you go everywhere by bicycle, and you can watch the horses roaming free on the plain.

The nearby island of Rügen, immortalized by the German Romantic painter Caspar David Friedrich, is frankly not to Erik's taste, and he tends to drag his heels when his parents go there for the weekend. Yet it is a delightful place, with wooden villas, white chalk cliffs, beech forests and little villages with thatched farmhouses. In a previous age, the British writer and adventurer Elisabeth von Arnim, a Pomeranian by marriage, used to come here in search of peace and quiet. But these tales of the past do not mean a whole lot to this young man, who prefers his unsophisticated little island by a long chalk.

PAGES 120–121: The barge's mooring, behind the dunes.

PAGE 122: The kitchen opens on to the main sitting room, where everyone likes to gather round the fire when the evenings are cool.

ABOVE AND OPPOSITE: Suspended between sky and sea, the barge rocks almost imperceptibly at its mooring, so calm is the Baltic in summer. When carrying out the restoration work, Steffi Weihrauch sought out the old furniture and well-worn materials that give the interior its unpretentious appearance.

Accommodation was needed for the two families who share the barge, hence the large number of bedrooms. All are very simply furnished, with just a few reminders that this is a boat and not a house.

LEFT: On the island of Hiddensee, people are ecologically minded. There is no access for cars, and everyone either uses a bicycle or walks.

Poland

Although most people still have a clear mental image of the shipyards at Gdańsk, from the dramatic days of Lech Walesa and the Solidarity movement, they know very little else about Poland's busy maritime capital. But refer to Gdańsk by its former name of Danzig, and a whole other set of associations springs to mind – the Free City, the granary of Europe, the trading centre that was crucial to the expansionist activities of the German merchants of the Hanseatic League. Situated at the mouth of the Vistula, its port has always been Pomerania's outlet to the sea – a state of affairs that continued right up to the 20th century, when the new port of Gdynia was built less than twenty kilometres away.

In the 14th century, Pomerania was under the control of the Teutonic Knights, eventually defeated with the help of the Polish King in the 15th century. The massive fortress of Marien-burg, or Malbork, former headquarters of the Grand Masters of the Order, is the continuing proof of their power and influence in that era. Danzig, although its fate was intimately bound up with the Hanseatic League, nevertheless enjoyed independent status, right up to the time of its annexation by Prussia in 1772, on the occasion of the second partition of Poland. The town briefly regained its privileged position as an independent city under the protection of Napoleon, and then once again in the 1920s.

Günter Grass, born in Danzig in 1927, remembers an age when the town was still essentially German, before World War II changed the course of its history. One thing that has not changed is the landscape of the great Pomeranian plain with its undulating fields of rye. Near Gdańsk, the coastal region is particularly attractive with gently sloping mountains.

PAGES 126–127: Fishing boats at Sopot.

OPPOSITE: A view of Gdańsk, where the houses line the banks of the river Vistula and the many canals crisscrossing the town.
RIGHT: Architectural details and a Baroque door reflect the Germanic past of the former Danzig.

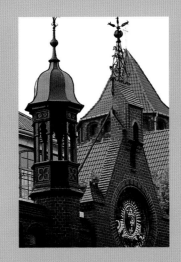

With its prestigious address on Heroes of Monte Cassino Street in Sopot, Eva and Michal's restaurant is the talk of the town.

Once upon a time, there was a doctor from Alsace serving in Napoleon's army called Jean Haffner, who believed that the waters of the Baltic Sea had healthgiving properties. This set him thinking about opening a spa on the outskirts of Danzig, and while the town was still under French protection, he acquired land in Sopot. Then, when the Empire fell and Prussian rule was restored, this same Dr Haffner built first his baths, in 1823, and in the following year a thermal spa, with beautiful parks and, above all, the big wooden pier which was to become the town's fashionable walking place and its principal landmark. As communications improved, with the building of a road and then a railway, which by 1870 extended to Warsaw, and finally the arrival of the Bornholm and Karlskrona steamboats, the German, Polish and Scandinavian aristocracy and wealthy bourgeoisie decided that this was the perfect place for a summer home. Blessed with beaches of fine sand and green hills, in the 1920s the resort once again enjoyed phenomenal success, benefiting now from the opening of a casino and the Grand Hotel.

Sopot began another chapter in its history in 1998, when it was refurbished as a spa and seaside resort within an independent Poland. For Eva and Michal Herman, this revival was the opportunity to realize a long-held dream of opening an art gallery where they would exhibit their own and their friends' work, their clientele drawn from passers-by in the town's quiet streets.

Eager to get started and make contacts, the two artists found the ideal location on Heroes of Monte Cassino Street, Sopot's main artery, and moved in. They soon realized that sitting there waiting for passing trade was just not their style. To attract visitors and provoke some sort of reaction, they turned the gallery into a restaurant, which they called the Blue Poodle (*Blekitny Pudel*) – the eccentric decor of which aroused comment from the start.

On the walls, mock family photos coexist with paintings ancient and modern, while the furnishings are more typical of a bohemian apartment than a restaurant. At the Blue Poodle, every object seems to celebrate the glories of Sopot in its heyday, no doubt appropriate now that the town's fortunes are again on the up and up....

PAGES 130–131: Even at the
entrance, the visitor is confronted
with an eclectic and incongruous mix
of objects. The street cobbles have
crept inside the house, and solid
doors are replaced with metal gates.

ABOVE AND OPPOSITE: Russian
wallpaper of a faded splendour,
armchairs upholstered with worn
leather, oil lamps, sewing machine,
telephone and transistor radio dating
from the days of recession – these
make up the old-fashioned decor
of the salon. These oddly familiar
objects evoke a powerful sense
of nostalgia.

OPPOSITE AND ABOVE: Amidst this
surreal assembly of bric-a-brac is
a collection of shoe lasts (above),
a bust of Karl Marx, a birdcage
and the cornice of an armoire, set
above a doorway. Portrait photos
and a few paintings by artist friends
fit perfectly into a decorative
scheme that has a curiously
haunting beauty (opposite).

Lithuania

The amber that washes on to the Baltic shores after a storm has always been regarded as a very mysterious thing: a gem that comes from water, with dead creatures trapped inside it. Much prized in antiquity, even in distant Greece, it was widely believed to have medicinal properties, and by the Middle Ages, the talismanic substance had become an important commodity, the subject of a trading monopoly controlled by the Teutonic Knights who occupied the coastal lands before overrunning Prussia.

Lithuania, which emerged as a state in the early 13th century, was viewed as a great prize by all the surrounding countries. In the 14th century, the capital Vilnius was established in the heartlands, not in the coastal region that was more exposed to the threat – and the actuality – of invasion. The country also sought to defend itself by uniting with Poland and adopting the Roman Catholic faith, a state of affairs that con-tinued until 1795, when Lithuania was incorporated into tsarist Russia. In the 19th and 20th centuries, it effectively shared the same fate as the other Baltic states.

Occupying the site of the Memelburg originally built by the Teutonic Knights, the port of Klaipeda has changed hands many times. The wind and sea have shaped the extraordinary geographical feature that confronts Klaipeda across the Courland Lagoon, that of the Curonian Spit, a long sandy isthmus curving like the blade of a foil, the southern part of which belongs to the Russian enclave of Kaliningrad. The German Expressionist painters were fascinated by its landscape of white sand dunes and pine forests, as too was Thomas Mann. These days, crowds of summer visitors are attracted here both by the landscape and the magical atmosphere of a place still touched by ancient pagan traditions and folklore.

PAGES 136–137: The jetty at the village of Nida on the Curonian Spit.

OPPOSITE AND RIGHT: Wood is omnipresent, and it is the principal material used in the construction of Lithuanian houses. On the edge of the pine forests stand old thatched farmhouses and pretty seaside villas, all brightly painted.

**A family of artists
was drawn to the
Curonian Spit by
its landscape of
windswept dunes.**

She was just twelve years old when she first went on holiday to the Curonian Spit. As a town-dweller, she thought then that living by the sea was a dream come true. When, many years later, Kristina and her husband Albertas Danilevicius went to the isthmus in the heart of winter to visit Kristina's best friend, whose ornithologist husband was observing the nesting habits of migratory birds on the peninsula, they decided almost then and there to leave behind their block of workers' flats in Vilnius, and swap the view of the neighbours' apartment for a view of the sea.

When they moved to Juodkrante nine years ago, it really did change their way of looking at the world. For Kristina, the best time of year to enjoy the landscape of windswept dunes is the winter, when silence is restored and a distinctive perfume fills the air. She loves to wander through the pine forests that anchor the fragile dunes and explore this improbable Baltic Sahara. Everything that comes from the sea holds a fascination for her, and the house is filled with pieces of driftwood that have been patinated by the waves. Seeds, branches and leaves, seaweeds and lichens collected locally constitute the materials for her work. For Kristina has, at least for the time being, given up her job as an art historian to concentrate on being an artist. She makes extraordinary compositions, collages of plant materials against a watercolour background, inspired by Turkish carpets. Albertas is a sculptor, and for him too pieces of wood found on the isthmus are a source of inspiration and pleasure. Every day their daughter Una takes the boat across to Klaipeda, where she is studying art with the intention of becoming a painter. Kristina now has plans to open a gallery of contemporary art in Juodkrante, dedicated to exhibitions of work by Baltic artists.

Thomas Mann was before them in finding inspiration on the peninsula. He built a little house there in the traditional style in which he spent two summers in the early 1930s; it is now a Thomas Mann museum. There are still many fine examples of thatched fishermen's cottages on this narrow tongue of sand between the lagoon and the sea. Kristina and Albertas live in a modern apartment, but the leafy branches of the tree outside their windows make it feel like a tree house. Every day as they look out, the view of Amber Bay convinces them all over again that they made the right decision in opting for a new life by the sea.

PAGE 140: The apartment occupies the top two floors of the building and appears to nestle among the trees that shade the balcony.

ABOVE AND OPPOSITE: The assorted items of furniture that give the apartment its bohemian air were passed on by neighbours in the nearby villages. And if you need to touch wood, this is the place to be because you are literally surrounded by it. It is Albertas Danilevicius's favourite material. He explains that he tries to put 'the soul of the wood' into his mysterious sculptures (opposite).

OPPOSITE: Grasses, twigs, leaves and seeds collected on the beaches or in the forest, washed by the waves and dried in the wind, are the elements from which Kristina Danilevicius creates her compositions. Set against a paper background washed with cool or sandy colour, the graphic interplay of the plant materials, simply glued on to the surface, evokes the landscape of the dunes and the grasses blowing in the wind.

ABOVE: On returning from her solitary and contemplative quests out in the bracing sea air, Kristina likes nothing more than to sit in front of the crackling fire, surrounded by objects from the natural world.

Latvia

The wild seashore of Courland falls away as a long ribbon of white sand on either side of the cape of Kolka, at the point where the waters of the Gulf of Riga emerge into the Baltic Sea. For hundreds of kilometres, there are just beaches lined with forests and the occasional little harbour with its colony of fishermen. A few still speak the Finno-Ugric of their Livonian ancestors, but that is becoming even rarer than the black storks that arrive in spring to nest in Latvia. The resort of Jurmala is today awakening from the long slumber into which it lapsed after the Russian elite's passion for sea-bathing came to an end. Cut off by the Lielupe river, the coastal strip boasts rows of pretty little wooden houses screened from the sea by pine trees.

Twenty-five kilometres away, Riga comes as an agreeable surprise. Dubbed the Paris of the Baltic, this Art Nouveau metropolis has a decidedly different look from the other Baltic capitals. The demolition of the outer walls that protected the Hanseatic Old Town, dominated by the castle of the Livonian Order, paved the way in the 19th century for the development of a modern town traversed by broad avenues and provided with attractive parks. Its location at the confluence of land, sea and river routes inevitably made it a thriving centre for trade and cultural exchange. The harbour at the mouth of the Daugava gives access to Russia's great rivers while, on the northern shore of the Gulf, the Via Baltica crosses the Baltic States and beyond.

PAGES 146–147: A view of Riga from Kipsala island.

OPPOSITE: The Vansu bridge links the centre of Riga with Kipsala island.
RIGHT: A Hanseatic house.
FAR RIGHT: A typical balcony in Jurmala, with dog, and a detail of a façade.

With the points
of the compass showing
your orientation,
the Captain's House
is the ideal spot
to drop anchor,
just over the bridge
from Riga.

Having spent the summer in their yacht touring the Åland islands in the Baltic Sea, Zaiga and Maris Gaile returned to Riga and moored in the Daugava. The idea suddenly came to them: why not live on the river bank and have the yacht moored right outside?

They soon narrowed their search to Kipsala island, whose old wooden houses and factories had long been left to rot, and their choice eventually lit on a plot with a wonderful garden. The house was falling apart, but Zaiga is an architect and Maris, who in 1995 was Prime Minister of Latvia, is a businessman. Neither was in the least fazed at the prospect of this massive project.

To preserve the neighbourhood's distinctive atmosphere, Zaiga has retained the main façade, which is built of wood, but made the interior resolutely modern. In the entrance hall, the points of the compass are drawn on the floor – situating the house within the cosmos. The library area and sitting room are on opposite sides of the imposing hearth that forms the central axis of the house. The bookshelves that occupy one whole wall, floor to ceiling, are readily accessible from the imposing staircase leading up to the bedrooms. Grabbing a book in passing and sitting down to read it on the stairs is part of the way of life.

With three grown-up children in the picture, the future use of the house was of paramount importance from the outset. Zaiga decided to divide up the space so that two families could live there at the same time, in the hope that one of the children would eventually move in with his or her own family. And that is exactly what has happened: their son has married and presented them with two grandchildren, non-identical twins, who live under the same roof. The Captain's House was very deliberately devised as a temporary port of call, a place for coming and going. In April 2003, Maris returned home from a two-year voyage that had taken him all over the world. Zaiga joined him for three legs of the journey, in French Polynesia, to Buenos Aires and to Cape Town. One incidental result is that a parrot from Chile has now joined the household.

With its wonderful view of old Riga – you can see the church towers out of the window – Kipsala soon became a fashionable location, 'over the bridge' from the town centre. Increasingly people are tempted to move somewhere where they can be surrounded by greenery, yet are only minutes by bicycle from the Old Town. Zaiga has an enviable reputation as an architect and regularly wins prizes for her work. She recently designed a hotel in Riga and is a prime mover in the development of a new residential quarter on the island. More of the old wooden houses are being done up and a former factory has been converted into loft spaces.

ABOVE AND OPPOSITE: Conceived according to the beliefs of the old Latvian peoples and the principles of the Indian mandala, the house has been designed around its energy centre. The precise position of the hearth was dictated by the route of an underground stream. It forms the vertical axis of the house with, to either side of it, the sitting room area (opposite) presided over by a grand piano and (above) the dining room with a table seating twenty-four.
RIGHT: The study wall displays a map of Riga and a picture of Kipsala island in the 19th century.

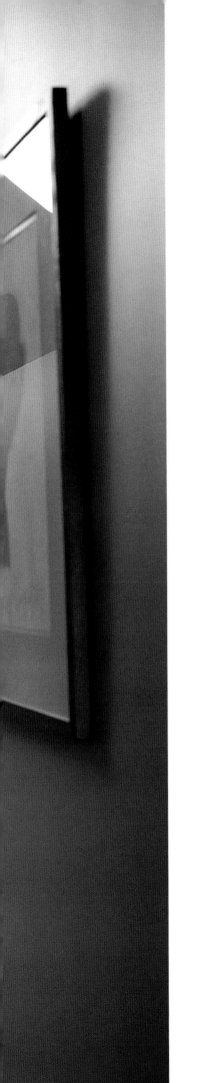

OPPOSITE: There is a definite flavour
of the cabin deck about this upstairs
corridor with its openwork doors
and yacht varnish on the oak floors –
a conscious or unconscious reference
to all the summers Zaiga and Maris
have spent on their boat.
RIGHT: The painting by Boris
Berzins is a good example of the
non-academic style of Latvian art.
It shares the space with a traditional
icon (above).

Estonia

Estonian manor houses are set deep within the forest, potent reminders of the days when the scions of the Baltic German aristocracy established in the region used to go hunting for brown bears, wild boar and lynxes. From 1238 to 1346, Estonia had been under Danish rule, before it was ceded to the Swordbrothers. Two hundred German merchants from Gotland were invited in to settle on the shores of the Gulf of Finland, their task to transform Tallinn ('town of the Danes') into a springboard for Hanseatic trade with Russia. Neither Swedish dominion in the 16th century nor rule by tsarist Russia from the 18th century caused more than a ripple in the estates held by the Baltic Germans, which continued to function as the granary for Western Europe.

Alas, few of the manor houses dating from Sweden's golden age escaped destruction in the Great War of the North in the early 18th century. A frenzy of reconstruction took place in the 18th and 19th centuries which tended to favour the neoclassical, neo-Renaissance, neo-Gothic and ultimately, in the early 20th century, Jugendstil or Art Nouveau.

While the rulers of the Baltic countries pursued their territorial squabbles, the Estonian peasants clung on both to their land and their Finno-Ugric language. Out in the countryside Estonian culture flourished, serving as a spearhead for national revival in the 19th century. The same ancestral tradition that resisted Nazi and Soviet oppression in the 20th century is today the guarantee of Estonia's independent identity within a wider Europe: this young nation is proud of its architectural heritage and eager to restore it to its former splendour.

PAGES 156–157: A view of Haapsalu Bay.

OPPOSITE: A villa in the resort of Haapsalu, once the favourite summer destination of the tsars, has now been turned into a restaurant.
RIGHT: A detail of a bow window in Tallinn's main street.
FAR RIGHT: Houses in Haapsalu.

With its long beaches
of fine white sand,
Pärnu Bay is popular
for seaside holidays,
but an artist couple
have chosen an
old farmhouse as
their summer home.

Like many dream homes, Sepamaa apparently chose its owners rather than the other way around, first luring them to the spot, then placing a few minor obstacles in their way to test the strength of their conviction, before surrendering itself unreservedly. And it did not choose just anyone: it chose an artist couple, Jaak Arro, a native of the region, and Epp Maria Kokamägi, who at once felt this was where she belonged. The old farmhouse, once the home of the village blacksmith (Sepamaa means 'home of the blacksmith'), was little more than a dilapidated ruin when the couple began bit by bit to domesticate it, back in those Soviet days when everything was in short supply.

Epp Maria is well known for her paintings of angels and has a passion for sky blue. Tongues began to wag in the village when she started to paint everything from the walls and doors to the floors and even the furniture in the very colour that was identified in people's minds with their former Russian occupiers. The Russians believed that if the door was blue, God would enter, and so they adopted the old Orthodox practice and used it as the colour for the doors and shutters of their homes. But Epp Maria stuck to her guns. At the time, it was far from easy to get hold of the materials needed to renovate the house: in the middle of a recession, it was a major endeavour to source the rolls of ancient gilded wallpaper that now cover the upper part of the walls.

For these two artists, one of the great things about the farmhouse was its stable, which they converted into a summer studio. As the light does not reach this magnificent space until the afternoon, the days tend to start gently with a bathe in the sea and a walk along the beach by the juniper trees, followed by breakfast cooked on the stove in the old-fashioned way. Maybe a few minutes in the garden tending the tomatoes and basil plants, then Epp Maria paints in the studio while Jaak sculpts in the garden. In the summer, the days are long and the light lasts forever. Friends come to share the unique atmosphere and sit around the samovar with them late into the night in the lamplight under the apple trees.

But their favourite time in Pärnu is Midsummer's Day. Epp Maria and her daughters put on traditional full red skirts for the occasion. Seven white flowers representing the birth of summer are slid under the girls' pillows, so they will see their future sweetheart in their dreams. It is the summer solstice, the longest day, and everyone is impatient for the night when big wood fires will be lit on the beach to frighten away evil spirits. Tradition has it that you burn an old boat, planting it upright in the sand so the flames leap high in the sky. Another favourite activity is catching fireflies, which Epp Maria compares to falling stars. Autumn always seems to come too soon, making them retreat indoors, where they have their own work and paintings by Epp Maria's parents for company.

ABOVE (TOP): Estonian farmhouses traditionally comprised a single long building on one level where animals and people lived adjacent to one another. The outer door led straight into the kitchen, which marked the division between living quarters and stable.

ABOVE (BOTTOM): A bas-relief by Jaak Arro leans against the stable wall. The comfortable proportions of these traditional farmhouses make them very much sought after today as second homes.

OPPOSITE: In summer, a wooden table and benches are set out under the branches of the big apple tree, creating an improvised dining room in the garden. If possible they like to eat all their meals in their 'outdoors room', often joined by the many friends who pass through – artists, writers and actors who appreciate the Chekhovian atmosphere.

ABOVE: Home to a painter, the old farmhouse displays the full gamut of colours. In the bedroom, panelling, floor and chairs are all painted sky blue, Epp Maria's favourite colour.
RIGHT: The sitting room benefits from warmer tones, browns and reds with ultramarine accents.
OPPOSITE: Until the autumn, the house is heated by two stoves: one modern, in heat-resistant stone, which Epp Maria uses for cooking; the other, with wrought-iron doors, used purely for warmth.

ABOVE AND OPPOSITE: In Estonia, it was the custom for women to wear different costumes according to their village of origin. With a strict code of dress distinguishing girls, married women and widows, there was a huge variety of styles. Even today the womenfolk of a small island off Pärnu wear their costume all the time, for fishing or for working in the fields.

On Midsummer's Day, Epp Maria and her daughters like to don their full striped skirts (above) for the traditional celebration of the summer solstice. The superb portrait of a peasant woman (above) is the work of Epp Maria's father, Luulik Kokamägi, while the large painting on the wall (opposite) was done by Epp Maria herself.

OPPOSITE AND RIGHT: 'The artists have taken over the cowshed!' exclaims Epp Maria with a laugh, referring to the summer studio in the converted stable (right). Once the doors are opened wide to let in the light, there is no real demarcation between inside and out, just a marvellous sense of freedom. This is where Epp Maria paints the angels for which she is famous, and Jaak sculpts his bas-reliefs, although he often prefers to work in the garden rather than clutter up the studio. Upstairs, a bedroom is installed in the well-lit, tranquil space that has been created underneath the handsome timber-frame roof (opposite and top right).

OVERLEAF: Sepamaa's private beach on Pärnu Bay.

On the Estonian island
of Saaremaa is a house
where two Finnish
sisters meet for
family get-togethers.

Ulla-Maija lives in Helsinki and Piri in Amsterdam.
One summer, when they were visiting their mother while she was convalescing at Pärnu, they discovered for themselves the charm of the Estonian coast. They began to think about buying a house where they could spend the holidays together, in the company of their family and friends. Back in Helsinki, Ulla-Maija learned that a small Finnish colony already existed on the island of Saaremaa (Osel in Swedish). The prime mover in the venture was the interior designer Ristomatti Ratia, a friend of hers. She called him at once to see if there just happened to be a house still available on the island.

When she first arrived in the garden of the house Ristomatti had told them about, Ulla-Maija was presented with the sight of a magnificent oak tree. It had to be an omen, as their family name was Tamminen, which means 'of oak'. Just two weeks later, Ulla-Maija and Piri took possession of an overrun plot planted with apple, cherry and nut trees, opening on to a field of orchids, and five minutes by bicycle from the sea.

Saaremaa had been used as a military base and was therefore cut off from the world during the years of Soviet occupation. As a result it had retained the rustic simplicity the sisters loved so much from the time they were children and used to spend the summers in a farmhouse in the southern part of Finland. There were the same scents, the same tasty vegetables, grown with the aid of manure from the kolkhoz or collective farm that was once next door. They began the task of restoring the house with the aid of Estonian workmen capable of making just about anything on the basis of a scribbled design – and who even spoke Finnish because of the Finnish radio and television broadcasts that had provided their only window on the world during the Soviet era.

As one holiday followed another, Piri and Ulla-Maija rediscovered the joys of a big family Christmas. Their children decorated a juniper tree with treasures they discovered for themselves, their mother plaited wreaths made of fir and laurel branches. Baltic herrings and the island's own sausages and beer figured on the menu. In the summer, the two sisters like an energetic tramp through the surrounding countryside and then, after a spot of gardening and a good lunch, they settle down in some favourite spot to while away the hours with a good book. As she looks out over the apple orchard, Ulla-Maija is currently tackling the voluminous diaries of Aino Kallas, a Finnish writer married to an Estonian man; she expects to finish them huddled in front of the fire in the New Year.

The rest of the time they are pretty busy. Their walks take them to interesting spots on the island, like a crater made by a meteorite, or a little moss-covered Romanesque church. They also help with a Waltz Festival held every summer near Kuressaare Castle, which was founded by the German Crusader Knights. As it happens, there is an old song called *The Saaremaa Waltz* that is still very popular in Finland and Estonia.

OPPOSITE AND ABOVE: It is a long journey from Helsinki – ferry, car, then boat to the small island of Muhu and across the bridge to Saaremaa. When the two sisters finally arrive and see their garden again, they feel they have earned their reward. Cool, shady and somewhat ramshackle, it is an idyllic spot to pass the summer out in the fresh air. It is customary for one or other of the little colony of Finns on the island to organize a garden party every year.

The pile of flat white stones (detail, opposite) is like a miniature version of the big Viking stone stacks that sailors used as landmarks in the days before lighthouses were invented. Inside the house, the sisters display these simple piles of stones as ornaments.

OPPOSITE: Finding chairs to go round the dining room table was a stroke of pure luck. Having seen just what they wanted on an old postcard, by complete chance they came across reproductions of the same thing in a shop window. They bore them off without even waiting for the second coat of paint!

ABOVE AND RIGHT: Piri grows her own vegetables under glass. She is also an excellent cook and adores her wood-burning range, built in the traditional style.

ABOVE, RIGHT AND OPPOSITE: In the former stable, now converted into a winter sitting-room (above and opposite), the fire burning brightly in the hearth is scented with juniper and pine cones (right). The walls are left plain, apart from a few framed photographs, a couple of shelves of books and, by the fire, a laurel wreath made for Christmas by Piri and Ulla-Maija's mother. Its counterpart is on the opposite wall: a beautiful funeral wreath (opposite) bought from an antique dealer on Saaremaa.

OPPOSITE AND ABOVE: The original of the ladder was spotted in an interior decoration magazine. The sisters had six of them made for hanging up towels and linen. The side table with branches for legs has been so successful that it is now being sold in a limited edition.

The sauna was based on a quick sketch by Ristomatti Ratia. The interior architect had been invited to dinner and simply drew it on a corner of the table while Piri was putting the finishing touches to the food.

You ladle water from the wooden bucket on to the hot stones until the temperature reaches 80°C, then beat yourself gently with a bundle of twigs previously immersed in water. Here oak twigs are used as a substitute for the more traditional birch.

Finland

If you are Finnish, it is not that unusual to have your very own island. This is because there are 95,000 of them in all shapes and sizes. One of the largest forms part of the autonomous province of Åland (Ahvenanmaa), an archipelago of 6,400 islands, but from anywhere in the Gulf of Bothnia or the Gulf of Finland your view out to the open sea will almost certainly be blocked by some rocky outcrop or wooded isle.

Over the centuries the inhabitants of the archipelagos have maintained strong links with Stockholm and Turku (Åbo), capital of the Finnish province that was once part of the kingdom of Sweden. From its medieval past Turku has retained not only its castle but the ancient custom of the long Christmas holiday. Addressing the townspeople on 24 December,

the mayor declares the start of celebrations that will go on until Twelfth Night. On the outskirts of the former capital a few quite exceptional manor houses illustrate the richness of Finland's architectural heritage.

In troubled times, as nationalism gained ground in the late 19th century, the Finns sought to define their national identity using nature, whose beauty was undimmed. The artists of this golden age found their primary source of inspiration in the forests, lakes and archipelagos, and wood and granite were the preferred materials of architects and designers. What distinguishes Finnish architecture today, apart from the striking harmony of its proportions, is its oneness with nature, the way it opens out into the natural world and blends with its surroundings.

PAGES 182–183: The heavily indented coastline of the Finnish mainland, seen from Oak Island.

OPPOSITE: Over half of Finland is covered in forest, and wood is the most frequently used material for traditional houses. Standing literally in the water, the typical red houses of Porvoo were originally warehouses.
FAR RIGHT: From the market in Helsinki.

Ekskär, or Oak Island,
is one hour by boat from
the Finnish mainland and
only a little further than
that from the Åland islands.

Heikki and Eeva-Kaarina Salmi were looking for a sheltered harbour where they could put in from time to time while they were out in their boat. Their choice lit on this tiny deserted island, and they determined to take the plunge and become the new owners. The island had previously been in continuous occupation over a period of three centuries, as home to successive generations of Swedish-speaking fishermen. There were traces of the very basic and harsh life they must have led – and in particular there was a tumbledown house and stable, whose solid stone walls would dictate the position and proportions of the new buildings designed by Eeva-Kaarina. Drawing not only on her experience as an architect but also on detailed study of traditional houses, she came up with some ingenious solutions. In the end she and Heikki opted for a low house built of squared-off logs in the Lapp style, with the emphasis on comfort and warmth; the island of Ekskär is a windy place out in the open sea and the only trees it supports are small and twisted, quite unsuitable for construction work or for heating on any major scale. The rooms radiate out from the central hearth and are intercommunicating to allow the heat to circulate freely. The children were given a house of their own.

The children's house incorporates the granite walls of the former stable. With its steeply pitched roof, it soon acquired the name 'the church'. To accommodate their large family, Heikki and Eeva-Kaarina created a sleeping area under the eaves. The extension to the church, which receives its outside light via a glazed screen wall, was soon dubbed 'the aquarium'. The church and aquarium are used all the time in summer but closed up in winter, when the occasional visitor will sleep on one of the benches in the main house – just as people used to do in the old farmhouses.

On the islands, everything has to be brought in by boat – with the exception of the fish that are in abundant supply in the Baltic Sea. In building the main house, Eeva-Kaarina and Heikki adopted a well-tried technique developed to suit Finland's particular geography, importing prefabricated modules from the mainland and then having them assembled on the island on the site of the old building.

White and soundless, the island looks quite different in winter. The couple recall arriving by car across the frozen sea to the nearest large island, then completing their journey on skis. The temperature may plummet, but it does not mean abandoning life in the open air. Wood still has to be chopped, and a hole cut in the ice allows you to fish, or indeed to indulge in the traditional practice of *avanto*, swimming in the icy sea. 'Just one small piece of advice,' insists Eeva-Kaarina. 'Wear woollen socks so your feet don't stick when you run naked over the ice!'

PAGES 186–187: An area of the aquarium, the annexe to the children's house.

OPPOSITE AND ABOVE: Long and low, the main house is inspired by the style of Lapp architecture. A terrace runs along the south-facing façade (above). The foundations were dug by local fishermen, and the chalet was then assembled more or less like a Lego kit. All the materials were brought in by boat, and the men lived under canvas while the work was done. There is another small terrace on the east side (opposite) that is sheltered from the wind, ensuring a sea view in all weathers.

Finland

OPPOSITE: Wood is the dominant material, inside and out, with few textiles to be seen. A softer note is introduced by sheepskins thrown over Kaare Klint's Safari chairs that grace the sitting-room.

ABOVE: One of the fundamental architectural principles in this part of the world is to use your energy sources economically. Solar power suffices for lighting, but only just; for heating, the main house relies on the fire in the hearth, which interconnects with the stove in the kitchen and a small wooden sauna.

RIGHT: On the terrace stand the big wooden casks once used as brine tubs by the fishermen, who used to pickle Baltic herring and sea birds for their own consumption.

ABOVE AND RIGHT: The objects left behind by the previous occupants make up a little museum collection of their own, including fishing nets, slippers of woven birch bark (above) and a wooden cask of the type used by sailors to store their clothes in the dry (right).

OPPOSITE: The granite stone walls of the old stable were incorporated into the children's house, known as the church. The simple yet effective table and chairs were made by Heikki. As in the main house, traditional rag runners decorate the floors. The stepladder up to the children's sleeping area was hewn out of a single tree trunk.

OPPOSITE (TOP): The smoke sauna has its origins in Finland's ancient shamanistic forests. Imported to the archipelago, it incorporates modifications to compensate for the shortage of wood. The roof hidden under its covering of grass is very nearly flat and the layer of plant material much thicker than would have been used on one of the old granaries. And there is no question here of separate compartments for smoking meat or fish, just a single space to which you can retire and enjoy a gentle perfumed warmth before plunging into the nearby sea. In summer the ceremony is performed daily, no doubt much to the delight of visitors who have dropped anchor for the night.

OPPOSITE (BOTTOM LEFT): The perforated planks of a fish tank, used by the fishermen who previously inhabited the island to transport live fish back to the shore.

ABOVE: The landing stage.

RIGHT: The spartan comforts of the outside toilet.

OVERLEAF: Facing south-west, the sheltered terrace has a view of the setting sun.

The manor house of Rilax (Riilahti) stands on raised ground on a promontory facing out to sea. That eminently strategic position betrays the military background of its designer, who did not give a fig that a north-easterly aspect was regarded as the least desirable in terms of light. At the dawn of the 19th century, in the absence of architects trained in Finland, it was an engineer in charge of fortifications, Pehr Grandstedt, who found himself entrusted with the building of the manor house. Erected between 1804 and 1806, just three years before Finland became a Russian Grand Duchy, it boasts a neoclassical portico and pediment, the very style that before long became the hallmark of the new capital of Helsinki.

There is a sense of unity about Rilax, which comes from the house and its contents being handed down through the generations.

Although the name Rilax makes you think of relaxation, it is more likely to come from the bay (or 'lax') down below. For Swedes and Finns, the name is synonymous with a major naval battle that took place there on 27 July 1714. And the history of Rilax manor is full of military associations. The first member of the Aminoff family to live there was Berndt Johan, who had been raised by a family of military officers in Moscow after his father was imprisoned and exiled to the Ural Mountains. He served first in a Russian regiment under the command of his adoptive father, and then in the Swedish army on the south-western tip of Finland. It was here he met Miss Körning, whom he married and who brought him Rilax as her dowry. The present manor house, however, was essentially the work of their grandson Johan Frederik, an intimate of King Gustav III; he also planted the park and built up a library that includes seventy volumes of the collected works of Voltaire. His son Adolf served as a general in the army of the Russian Grand Duchy of Finland. When he returned home he had his bedroom hung with *trompe-l'œil* wallpaper to make it look like a soldier's tent.

If a military career brought the family honours and distinction, the estate with its fields and forests provided a far from negligible source of income. Wood was taken away by boat to provide fuel for the stoves of Stockholm and Tallinn. *The Delphine* was one of two boats owned by General Adolf in the late 19th century, and used to carry goods from the estate as far as the North Sea. The sea was of course the obvious route out of Rilax. The current owner recalls how in the 1920s he used to go by sea to Hanko to catch the train to Helsinki, where he was a student. Latterly, for this enthusiastic sailor and his children, the sea has come to represent adventure, the high point of unforgettable holidays spent at Rilax.

PAGE 198: A view of General Adolf's rooms. A collection of swords, rifles and military engravings is displayed on the walls, while a model of a ship hangs down from the revealed beams that give the room its rustic air.

ABOVE AND OPPOSITE: When Finland fell to Russia in 1809, the Aminoffs, whose Russian origins can be traced back as far as the 17th century, came once again under the Tsar's authority. Alexander I ennobled the family, granting them the title of Count.

The apartments occupied by General Adolf, who served in the army of the Russian Grand Duchy of Finland, date from the second half of the 19th century. These attic rooms have their walls lined with blue fabric and are decorated in the Russian style, with the dark, intricately carved furniture that was in vogue in the General's day.

ABOVE AND OPPOSITE: Johan Frederik
was held in prison for two years
following the assassination of King
Gustav III in 1792. He subsequently
returned to his estates, where
he oversaw the work on his new
manor house.

On the piano nobile, his
furnishings have survived the
modernization of the decorative
scheme undertaken, with
considerable sensitivity, by his son
General Adolf. In these discreetly
wallpapered rooms, all the graceful
decorum of the original has been
preserved, and the white Gustavian
pieces are perfectly complemented
by their Biedermeier counterparts.

The lovely parquet floors of Svartå Manor (Musto) merit your utmost respect and admiration. They comprise four different species of wood and are regularly waxed, never varnished. Through the centuries, the occupants of the house have always worn felt slippers indoors (except when entertaining). Everyday life at the manor house was not at all grand, and not that different from village life. Meat and fish were rarely on the menu, and the curtains were more likely to have been linen than silk or velvet. In a country where the darkness is so oppressive in winter, the real luxury was the number of windows, on which a duty was paid to the Swedish crown. Their double glazing was an innovation at the time, helping to retain the heat from the tiled stoves installed in the reception rooms.

Built of wood and faced with pilasters and pediments, this elegant building was visited by many Swedish kings and Russian tsars, who wanted to express their esteem for and confidence in the Linders, owners of the estate and its forges since the 18th century. Effectively, the history of the manor is the history of this family and its Finnish foundries.

The Royal Forges of Svartå were originally administered by Sweden, and one day a Swedish inspector happened to visit. His name was Magnus Linder, and he knew how to make himself agreeable to the owner, a Baltic German called Henrik Johan Kreij. He married his daughter a few years later. Their son Magnus Linder II built the manor house. Two architects, Christoffer Friedrich Schröder and Erik Palmstedt, were summoned, one from Åbo (Turku) and the other from Stockholm, and together were commissioned to build an ochre-coloured dwelling house appropriate to serve as the family mansion. As a finishing touch, a statue of Diana was erected in the Baroque gardens.

Set in beautiful gardens, Svartå Manor is a haven of peace where time stands still.

Magnus Linder III went away to study at Uppsala in Sweden. By the time he returned to Finland in 1810, it had become a Russian Grand Duchy. In Russia, the Finnish forges found a new outlet, and at the same time Magnus's son Fridolf obtained a position in the service of the Governor-General of Finland. Svartå's wonderful neogothic follies are a legacy of this period. In the gardens, by then laid out in the English style, stables and a coach house were designed by the architect Anders Fredrik Granstedt. With their rose windows and spires, they actually looked more like Gothic chapels, although this style is curiously absent from the history of Finnish architecture.

The stables fell into disrepair some fifty years later with the arrival of the first car ever to be seen in Finland. It was imported from France, together with its chauffeur, by the fiery Hjalmar Linder, who managed to ruin himself within the space of three years. In 1985, the Linder family kept faith with their illustrious ancestors by buying back the family home and starting the task of restoring it to its former condition.

PAGES 204–205: The English-style
gardens with their lake.
PAGE 206: A view of the ballroom.

ABOVE: In the early years of the
20th century, Hjalmar Linder (in the
painting above) was the richest man
in the country. Being an impassioned
defender of the working classes, who
were on the losing side when the
Reds were defeated in Finland's
civil war, he was obliged to leave the
country. With the help of Russian
aristocrats living in exile since the
Bolshevik Revolution, he managed
to squander his fortune, travelling all
over Europe on his private train.
OPPOSITE: In the ballroom, the *trompe-
l'œil* wall decorations – fluted
columns, medallions, braziers and
niches with statues, of the type
fashionable at the Swedish court at
the end of the 18th century – were
executed after drawings by the
manor's architect Erik Palmstedt.

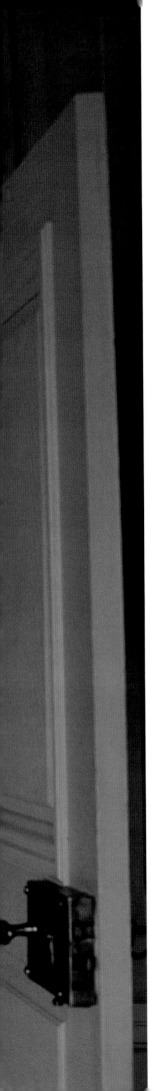

OPPOSITE: When Magnus Linder II moved to Svartå with his young wife in 1783, only the ground floor was habitable. The Gustavian furniture, although subsequently added to, dates largely from the period of their occupation.

ABOVE: The elegant table in the dining room recalls the grand dinners of the period, at which distinguished visitors would be served Madeira and fine wines.

RIGHT: However much they might have liked costly parquet and silk curtains, the norm was making do with linen and pine planks with a squared design in imitation of a parquet floor.

ABOVE AND OPPOSITE: The Linder family are the owners of a major art collection, evidence both of their social rank and excellent taste. Baron Fridolf Linder was an enthusiastic archaeologist who in the second half of the 19th century collected more than three hundred Stone Age objects, which he left to the museum in Turku.

Hjalmar Linder covered the walls of the manor house with some distinguished works of art, including paintings by Rembrandt and Joshua Reynolds. He was a generous patron to Finnish painters of the late 19th century, purchasing Albert Edelfelt's *White Queen* and commissioning work from his brother-in-law, Louis Sparre. In the 1920s, he presented his valuable collections to the Finnish Museum of Fine Arts.

It is a legendary house created by a legendary couple, Antti and Vuokko Nurmesniemi, two figures at the forefront of Nordic style in the 1960s and 1970s – one as an architect, the other as a designer, working in fashion, glass and ceramics. The house was built when they were at the peak of their success, and it remains quite unchanged; even the paintings are original. Yet it is not that the house has become marooned in the past, rather that it has become a design classic, a style archetype. The huge bright space, with large glazed bays, and the waxed blond wood of Finnish forests interact with its environment. So perfectly thought through and executed that nothing has been modified over the years and nothing added except a library.

Antti Nurmesniemi was taking a huge gamble. A house that was 500 metres square: a single space with no internal dividing walls, except for the bedroom, and put together like an industrial building, with twelve pillars and a steel frame. When the first snow arrived and lasted several weeks, Antti got worried and called the foreman: 'Call back if it's still snowing in six months,' came the reply. In the event, the flat roof (a bold stroke in the northern Baltic) has never once leaked. In those years of oil shortages, Antti was also worried about the loss of heat in such a large space. Triple glazing was installed and underfloor heating as well as radiators, but it has never been used. And similarly the air conditioning, introduced in case the building overheated like a greenhouse, has also proved superfluous.

So, a single volume, with virtually no doors or partitions. The living spaces – entrance hall, dining room, kitchen, sauna and living room – are subtly demarcated by differences of level. Everything is calculated to the nearest millimetre, including the furniture. Few objects, and those that do exist are hidden away in cupboards that are rarely opened. Not many pictures, and not because there are few walls to hang them on, but because they would seem almost incongruous in this open space.

With its unencumbered outlook, nature and the sea are much in evidence. After ten summers, Antti and Vuokko parted with their old holiday home, certain that Kulosaari (Brandö) was the place for them. Perhaps because together they had created the modern equivalent of something architects had dreamed of as far back as the late 19th century: a garden city, where the Swiss chalet look was abandoned in favour of houses built of the Art Nouveau materials of brick and stone, so that they could be lived in all year round.

For Vuokko, as she talks about her island, the house is filled with memories of her husband Antti. With its parks where you can ski in winter and a casino with one of the finest views of Helsinki, Kulosaari is an exceptional place to live, just a few minutes from the town centre. 'Do you know,' she adds, 'that in winter the connections are even quicker, because the buses go from island to island over the frozen sea? Finland is the only country in the world where you can do that.'

A garden city on the Helsinki archipelago, Kulosaari offers all the pleasures of living by the sea in the heart of the capital.

PAGE 215: Originally designed in 1952 by Antti Nurmesniemi for Helsinki's Palace Hotel, the stools in the sauna have become huge bestsellers. Inspired by the three-legged stools traditionally used for milking, their combination of extreme formal simplicity with natural wood has made them modern icons.

RIGHT: Most of the seating was designed by Antti.
OPPOSITE: On the floor above, a space for relaxation. One of the walls has been replaced by a series of glazed bays, an architectural solution that encourages the sense of being at one with nature.

PAGES 218–219: The dining room
has the same minimalist decor as
the rest of the house. It occupies
the intermediate level and adjoins
the kitchen.

ABOVE: With its starkly geometric
lines, the pine staircase inhabits its
space like a sculpture. Reduced to its
simplest expression, the ramp turns
into a shelf at the base. On the bench,

a hat, a souvenir of Vuokko's early
days when she was a designer for
Marimekko. In the boutique that
bears her name on the Esplanade
in Helsinki, Vuokko still displays her
brightly coloured fashions.

OPPOSITE: After a sauna and a few
reviving lengths in the swimming
pool, relaxation is the theme in the
adjacent seating area, which is
situated below sea level.

Sølvi dos Santos would like to express her deepest thanks to all those people, often complete strangers, who opened the doors of their homes to her and helped her in every way possible. This book is dedicated to them as an expression of her sincere gratitude.

Translated from the French, *Maisons de la Baltique*, by Jane Brenton

Any copy of this book issued by the publisher as a paperback is sold subject to the condition that it shall not by way of trade or otherwise be lent, resold, hired out or otherwise circulated without the publisher's prior consent in any form of binding or cover other than that in which it is published and without a similar condition including these words being imposed on a subsequent purchaser.

First published in the United Kingdom in 2005 by Thames & Hudson Ltd, 181A High Holborn, London WC1V 7QX

www.thamesandhudson.com

First paperback edition 2009

British Library Cataloguing-in-Publication Data
A catalogue record for this book is available from the British Library

ISBN 978-0-500-28843-6

Printed and bound in China by SNP Leefung Printers Limited